Dreamers

Yuyi Morales

NEAL PORTER BOOKS

HOLIDAY HOUSE / NEW YORK

I dreamed of you,
then you appeared.
Together we became

Amor—
Love—
Amor.

Resplendent life, you and I.

One day
we bundled gifts
in our backpack,

and crossed a bridge
outstretched like the universe.

Adiós Corazón

And when we made it
to the other side,
thirsty, in awe,

unable to go back,
we became immigrants.

Migrantes,
you and I.

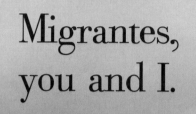

The sky and the land
welcomed us in words
unlike those of
our ancestors.

There were so many things
we didn't know.
Unable to understand
and afraid to speak,

we made lots of mistakes.

You and I
became caminantes.

Thousands and thousands of steps
we took around this land,
until the day we found . . .

a place we had
never seen before.

Suspicious.

Improbable.

Unbelievable.

Surprising.

Unimaginable.

Where we didn't need to speak,
we only needed to

trust.

And we did!

Books became our language.
Books became our home.
Books became our lives.

We learned to read,

and
to make
our voices heard.

Someday we will become
something we haven't even
yet imagined.

But right now . . .

We are stories.
We are two languages.
We are lucha.
We are resilience.
We are hope.

We are dreamers,
soñadores of the world.

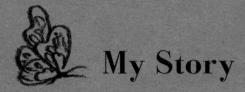

My Story

All of us have stories. Each of them is different. *This* story began in 1994, when I crossed a bridge with my two-month-old son, Kelly, from Ciudad Juarez, Mexico, to El Paso, Texas—and, though I did not know it at the time, to a new life in a strange and unfamiliar place, the United States of America. Once here, I was surprised by the quietness of the streets, the houses neatly lined up along the roads, and, later, by the cold winds of San Francisco Bay in summer. I had come so that my son could meet his great-grandfather Ernie, who was very ill and not expected to live much longer, and to marry Kelly's father, a US citizen. I wanted to return to Mexico soon afterward, but was shocked to learn that because of US immigration rules and my new status as a "permanent resident," I was now expected to remain in the United States. I had become an immigrant. But could I possibly call this new place my home?

Like most immigrants, I missed things that felt familiar: my family, the food, my friends, my job as a swimming coach, and my ability to communicate—to understand and be understood. In this new place where I did not speak the language, it was as if no one seemed to notice I existed, as if my words and actions didn't count. In those first days, I constantly wondered if I would ever find a place where I felt valued.

Then one day Kelly's grandmother brought us to a building that would change our lives forever. We discovered the public library, and it was SPECTACULAR!

I had never been in a place where you could just take books from the shelves without asking and without being scolded for taking them. And there were *picture* books, something I had not encountered before. I could not believe how beautiful and sturdy they were—and then, when I opened them, I was amazed at the power of their illustrations. Even though I could understand very few of the words, I realized that I could understand the story through those images—a realization that would come to inspire me later on. I began bringing Kelly there almost every day, and although at first it was difficult for a little baby to stay longer than a few minutes, eventually we were able to spend entire afternoons looking at picture books, often only leaving when we were told the library was closing. We were at home.

During those years, as Kelly got older, librarians at the Western Addition Branch, Richmond Branch, Presidio Branch, Mission Branch, and the San Francisco Main Library on Larkin Street, among many others, guided Kelly and me to find books we could love, though in an English that I struggled to understand. One day, when Kelly was not yet two years old, Nancy Jackson, the children's librarian at the Western Addition Branch, handed him his own library card. I was in awe! We could now take home a stroller brimming with books.

One of the most important things I learned at the library is that through books we can find our path and our purpose. I also learned that I love to tell stories, and that I could tell them through books. I studied the books I admired so much and became determined to make my own. My first efforts were very simple and very crude, made by hand and bound with ribbons and filled with my own stories and drawings. I was so proud of those books!

Kelly was not a *Dreamer* in the way the word is used today, to refer to young undocumented immigrants who were brought to the United States as children, and who have lived and gone to school here and know no other country than this one as their own. Kelly and I were Dreamers in the sense that all immigrants, regardless of our status, are Dreamers: we enter a new country carried by hopes and dreams, and carrying our own special gifts, to build a better future. **Dreamers** and **Dreamers of the world, migrantes soñadores.**

Now I have told you my story. What's yours?

Yuyi

Books That Inspired Me (and Still Do)

Ada, Alma Flor. *Under the Royal Palms*. New York: Atheneum, 1998.

Aliki. *Manners*. New York: Greenwillow Books, 1990.

Anzaldúa, Gloria, illustrated by Maya Christina Gonzalez. *Prietita and the Ghost Woman / Prietita y la Llorona*. Bilingual edition. San Francisco: Children's Book Press, 2001.

Argueta, Jorge, illustrated by Elizabeth Gómez. *A Movie in My Pillow / Una película en mi almohada*. Bilingual edition. San Francisco: Children's Book Press, 2001.

Burningham, John. *Granpa*. New York: Crown, 1984.

Burningham, John. *John Patrick Norman McHennessy: The Boy Who Was Always Late*. New York: Crown, 1987.

Byars, Betsy, illustrated by Marc Simont. *My Brother, Ant*. New York: Viking, 1996.

Cisneros, Sandra. *Woman Hollering Creek and Other Stories*. New York: Random House, 1991. Cover painting by Nivia Gonzales.

Crews, Donald. *Freight Train*. New York: Greenwillow Books, 1978.

Crews, Donald. *Shortcut*. New York: Greenwillow Books, 1992.

Curtis, Christopher Paul. *The Watsons Go to Birmingham—1963*. New York: Delacorte Press, 1995.

Engle, Margarita, illustrated by Sean Qualls. *The Poet Slave of Cuba: A Biography of Juan Francisco Manzano*. New York: Henry Holt and Company, 2006.

Gantos, Jack. *Joey Pigza Loses Control*. New York: Farrar, Straus and Giroux, 2000. Jacket art by Beata Szpura.

Garza, Carmen Lomas. *In My Family / En mi familia*. Bilingual edition. San Francisco: Children's Book Press, 2000.

Harris, Robie H., illustrated by Michael Emberley. *It's Perfectly Normal: Changing Bodies, Growing Up, Sex, and Sexual Health*. 4th ed. Somerville, MA: Candlewick, 2014.

Herrera, Juan Felipe, illustrated by Elly Simmons. *Calling the Doves / El canto de las palomas*. Bilingual edition. San Francisco: Children's Book Press, 1995.

Herrera, Juan Felipe, illustrated by Elizabeth Gómez. *The Upside Down Boy / El niño de cabeza*. Bilingual edition. San Francisco: Children's Book Press, 2000.

Hopkins, Lee Bennet, illustrated by Charlene Rendeiro. *Been to Yesterdays: Poems of a Life*. Honesdale, PA: Boyds Mills Press, 1995.

Jiménez, Francisco. *The Circuit: Stories from the Life of a Migrant Child*. Albuquerque: University of New Mexico Press, 1997.

Kalman, Maira. *What Pete Ate from A to Z*. New York: G. P. Putnam's Sons, 2001.

Kasza, Keiko. *A Mother for Choco*. New York: G. P. Putnam's Sons, 1992.

Moss, Lloyd, illustrated by Marjorie Priceman. *Zin! Zin! Zin! A Violin*. New York: Simon & Schuster, 1995.

Nye, Naomi Shihab, illustrated by Nancy Carpenter. *Sitti's Secrets*. New York: Simon & Schuster, 1994.

Nye, Naomi Shihab. *The Tree Is Older Than You Are: A Bilingual Gathering of Poems & Stories from Mexico*. New York: Simon & Schuster, 1995. Jacket art by Leticia Tarragó.

Priceman, Marjorie. *Emeline at the Circus*. New York: Alfred A. Knopf, 1999.

Rabinowitz, Alan, illustrated by Catia Chien. *A Boy and a Jaguar*. Boston: Houghton Mifflin Harcourt, 2014.

Rappaport, Doreen, illustrated by Shane W. Evans. *No More!: Stories and Songs of Slave Resistance*. Somerville, MA: Candlewick Press, 2001.

Rathmann, Peggy. *Officer Buckle & Gloria*. New York: G.P. Putnam's Sons, 1995.

Robertson, David Alexander, illustrated by Julie Flett. *When We Were Alone*. Winnipeg: HighWater Press, 2017.

Sáenz, Benjamin Alire, illustrated by Esau Andrade Valencia. *A Perfect Season for Dreaming / Un tiempo perfecto para soñar*. Bilingual edition. El Paso, TX: Cinco Puntos Press, 2008.

Santiago, Chiori, illustrated by Judith Lowry. *Home to Medicine Mountain*. San Francisco: Children's Book Press, 1998.

Shannon, David. *No, David!* New York: Scholastic, 1998.

Sharmat, Marjorie Weinman, illustrated by Marc Simont. *Nate the Great.* New York: Coward-McCann, 1972.

Simont, Marc. *The Stray Dog.* New York: HarperCollins, 2001.

Sís, Peter. *A Small Tall Tale from the Far Far North.* New York: Alfred A. Knopf, 1993.

Sís, Peter. *Madlenka's Dog.* New York: Farrar, Straus and Giroux, 2002.

Soto, Gary. *Baseball in April and Other Stories.* San Diego: Harcourt, 1990. Cover illustration by Barry Root.

Soto, Gary, illustrated by Susan Guevara. *Chato's Kitchen.* New York: Putnam, 1995.

Steig, William. *Amos & Boris.* New York: Farrar, Straus and Giroux, 1971.

Steig, William. *Doctor De Soto.* New York: Farrar, Straus and Giroux, 1982.

Steptoe, John. *Stevie.* New York: Harper and Row, 1969.

Stevenson, James. *The Mud Flat Olympics.* New York: Greenwillow Books, 1994.

Tan, Shaun. *The Arrival.* New York: Arthur A. Levine / Scholastic: 2007.

Teague, Mark. *Dear Mrs. LaRue.* New York: Scholastic, 2002.

Van Draanen, Wendelin. *Sammy Keyes and the Hotel Thief.* New York: Alfred A. Knopf, 1998. Jacket art by Dan Yaccarino.

Whybrow, Ian, illustrated by Tony Ross. *Little Wolf's Book of Badness.* Minneapolis: Carolrhoda Books, 1999.

Young, Ed. *Lon Po Po: A Red-Riding Hood Story from China.* New York: Philomel, 1989.

Yumoto, Kazumi. *The Friends.* Translated by Cathy Hirano. New York: Farrar, Straus and Giroux, 1996. Jacket art by Tatsuro Kiuchi.

Publication information is for first American edition unless otherwise indicated. Reprint editions may be available from other publishers.

To Dreamers of all kinds, especially those who have brought their abundant gifts to a new land—you are the inspiration for this book

How I Made this Book

I painted with acrylics and drew on paper with ink and brushes and a nib pen that once belonged to Maurice Sendak, given to me by Lynn Caponera. To give the book life, I photographed and scanned many things, including: the floor of my studio • the comal where I grill my quesadillas • my childhood drawings kept by my mother • a chair • a brick from my house • old walls from the streets of Malinalco, my hometown of Xalapa, and my house • a metal sheet • traditional Mexican fabrics • crepe, craft, and amate papers • leaves and plants from my garden • an old woven blouse • hand-painted pants I made for my son, Kelly • old wood • water in a bucket • jute twine • a traditional wool skirt from Chiapas • Kelly's childhood drawings • my first handmade book • embroidery • and more.

Neal Porter Books

Text and illustrations copyright © 2018 by Yuyi Morales
All Rights Reserved
HOLIDAY HOUSE is registered in the U.S. Patent and Trademark Office.
Printed and Bound in May 2018 at Toppan Leefung, Dong Guan City, China.
www.holidayhouse.com
First Edition
10 9 8 7 6 5 4 3 2 1

Library of Congress Cataloging-in-Publication Data is available.